T0144952

LEARNING IS GRAND

And Other Poems & Stories

Written by

LOIS LUND

Illustrated by

ANNETTE EADIE

AuthorHouse™
1663 Liberty Drive
Bloomington, IN 47403
www.authorhouse.com
Phone: 1 (800) 839-8640

© 2015 Lois Lund. All rights reserved.

No part of this book may be reproduced, stored in a retrieval system,
or transmitted by any means without the written permission of the author.

Published by AuthorHouse 07/26/2019

ISBN: 978-1-4969-6872-2 (sc)
ISBN: 978-1-4969-6873-9 (e)

Print information available on the last page.

Any people depicted in stock imagery provided by Thinkstock are models,
and such images are being used for illustrative purposes only.
Certain stock imagery © Thinkstock.

This book is printed on acid-free paper.

Because of the dynamic nature of the Internet, any web addresses or links contained in this book may have changed
since publication and may no longer be valid. The views expressed in this work are solely those of the author and do
not necessarily reflect the views of the publisher, and the publisher hereby disclaims any responsibility for them.

authorHOUSE®

DEDICATIONS

I Want to Thank My husband who has supported me.
I also want to thank my friend Annette
Eadie for her excellent artwork.
I want to thank Sam Quin, and Andrea Adonis, for
their invaluable assistance in forming this book.
I'd like to thank my Daughter for her efforts too. I'd
like to give special credit to my nurse who has given
me credit and inspiration for this project.

This has been a feat to undertake this on a Saturday with Sunday
coming up and church, Tomorrow. It has kept busy and at times
almost stalemated. But the book was meant to be. Sunday also
will be here and I will sleep tonight. It has been a very busy day.

Thank you God my Father for watching over me.

CONTENTS

BABY CHICK

As yellow as butter
Like a new cotton ball
Is the new baby chick
With it's cheep-cheeping call

It's sparkly black eyes
Are as round as can be
As I hold it so gently
And then set it free

To run all about with it's
Little orange feet
Pecking at grain bits
I give it to eat.

Dear little chicken
You're one of the things
I'm glad that the
Coming of Easter time brings!.

SQUIRREL

He scampers so quickly
This lively young squirrel.
His tail is so fluffy
It's always in curl.

He never makes noise
Unless somethings the matter,
Then you will hear a noise like a chatter.

He likes to eat peanuts, acorns and pecans underground.
He goes up a tree trunk
Then down and 'round.

It's so special to see one
'cause he is so bright.
He sees you first
Then he's outa' sight.

3

LEAP FROG

Green as a leaf
On a big shady tree
Is the new little froggie
Look closely to see

He knows how to creep
In his home on the ground
And makes a big leap
That's how he gets 'round.

Patient he must be
Although he is young
To catch a big fly
With his long sticky tongue.

The thing about froggies
Is that they can leap
That's why when you catch one
He's so hard to keep.

HANDS AND TOYS

Your hands are your friends;
Eight fingers, two thumbs.
With them you play
And have lots of fun.

Your toys are your tools
To learn how to do.
Some come in boxes
Do you play with them too?

Hands are for holding
Sometimes it's important.
They're good for folding;
A time to be reverent.

Please boys and girls
At the end of your play
Please pick up your toys
And put them away.

5

GOOD MORNING

Good morning!
A brand new day!
Still in your pajamas
What's going on today?

Remember what mom said.
Help her make your bed.

Is Teddy bear near?
Clothes out to wear.

Had a good rest.
Pray before breakfast..

Help mom when you can.
Make someone happy today.
You'll be tired at the end of day.

We love you. God Bless You.

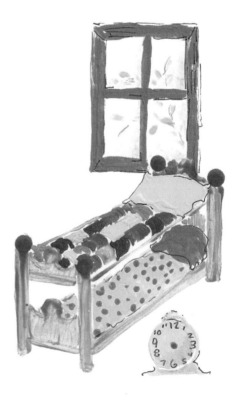

DAY BEFORE SCHOOL

Tomorrow morning It's time to go to school.
I put my clothes out the night before.
I need socks and shoes for the morning.
To tie my shoes one at a time
Here is a lesson:
Make a single tie and pull it tight.
Pull up one string and make a loop
Hold the loop as I pull the other string
Around that loop.
You push the other string
Through the first loop making a 2nd loop
Then I pull both loops snug and tight.
It takes practice.
Now you do the same thing
With your other shoe.
NOW YOU CAN RUN!!

SNOW

Nature's snow is a beautiful thing. It's a wonder.
It stays on top of things in a beautiful landscape.
It's just so pretty! It snow's at 32
degrees outside or colder.

Wear warm mittens and a warm coat. If it's real
cold real cold I won't pack or make a snowball.
If it's not so cold you can make a snow ball.
Make a fort and fill it with snowballs to throw.

Pack the snow and make a snow man. Roll and
roll the snow into a big ball. To make a snowman's
head. Another bigger ball for his tummy and
a bigger ball all of snow for his base.

Dress him up he needs eyes, a nose and
a mouth, He needs a hat to keep his head
warm and a scarf around his neck.

LEARNING IS GRAND

1234 AND 5
HAVE YOU HEARD OF A HONEY BEE HIVE?

1234567
DO YOU KNOW HOW A SOUL GOES HEAVEN?
JESUS AND ANGELS WELCOME HIM THERE.
IT WILL BE FAR BETTER THAN THE FAIR.

ABCDEFG
JESUS DIED FOR YOUR SIN. DON'T YOU SEE?
HIS RIGHTEOUSNESS TO WIN.
HE'S AT THE DOOR OF YOUR HEART JUST ASK HIM IN.

12345678910
TO LEARN ABOUT NUMBERS THERE IS NO END.
WITH THEM YOU CAN DO WONDERS.

HIJKLMNOPQR NOW YOU CAN LEARN THIS JUST SAY IT AGAIN
HIJKLMNOPQ R FOR ROSES

STUVW XY FOR XYLOPHONE
THEN Z IS THE LAST
AND IT IS FOR ZEBRA.

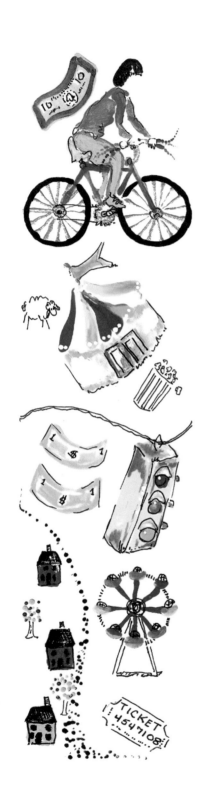

BICYCLE

by Lois Lund

It was new, it was blue, 24 inch wheels.
White handles and colored streamers.
As soon as you balanced
You ride with no hands.

Small town 1960s
The streets and allys were mine.
My brother went his way.
I was cruisin' in Greentown, USA

Population 2500
One traffic light
But you didn't need to ride
On Main street.

The County Fair was in the fall.
My haircut style was the Beatles.
I had $12.00 to spend
And it was enough.

I went with a friend.
It wasn't hot there!
We rode the bullet
I turned backwards and upside down!
Scream and whoa!
I laughed.

MUSIC

Do you know how to sing?
Playing a musical instrument
Is a wonderful thing.
When you learn how to play
It's a God-Given talent.

I don't play piano or flute
Or saxaphone or clarinet
I play the trumphet and I love it
Or trombone or drums
Just do what you do
The best that you can.

You'll probably be in the band
When you go to school
That's really great too.
Congratulations! I'm rooting for you.

FEEDING THE DUCKS

August 2014

Oh, there are swans, ducks and birds at Lake Eola.

They are so tame because so many people go there.
Two black swans, white swans with two foot long
necks. Beautiful really but he wanted more than bread
he tried to bite my gold ring. They were hungry!

There were colorful ducks with yellow bills. Many white
birds with pink legs, feet and beaks, and beautiful oscillating
eyes. That means they were round black and yellow eyes
with white eyelids covering down around each eye.

Then it was sprinkling rain and the wind blew very hard.

My friend's umbrella blew inside out. It was fun.

MONEY

Do you get paid money for chores that you
do? You can ask for allowance.
That's a good balance.

If you can sew or climb up a ladder there's things you can do
Something's always needs done, whit whoo!

You can paint or you can sew pillows,
wash cars or wash windows
Iron clothes or clean garages. Parents would appreciate
If you took out the garbage.

Be creative about things that you can do and
don't be shy Just put your best foot forward
and interact with others. Ask for your pay.
It's not rude to say.

A girl got a job just the other day. She asked me to pray.

To learn its value and what you would like
Don't spend just for pop and candy
But save for a bike.

For every dollar God says give a dime
He'll bless you with more
He honors your tithe.
It's a great lesson that you can learn
Get ready for blessings
From Him in return.

TESTS IN SCHOOL

Hello student!
You will learn to read, learn to write, and learn arithmetic too.
You will have tests in school.
But it's not so difficult.

Western civilization has always had vigorous testing.
For students. This is not to harm you or alarm you.
Pay attention to your classes
Listen to your teacher. Read your books; read slowly to
to get the concept if it's difficult. Test yourself as you read.
And pray when you need to. God hears you!

Play a musical instrument for activity, sing, or do sports.
Choose your friends wisely.

If you can't read. Get help. Someone will help you.
Don't be afraid to ask your teacher. It might take you
more time to learn reading but you will always be happy you did.
You can make good grades and do extra activities for fun.
Like when you need money you can work. It's important to read
if you want to earn money.
In America everyone can learn to read. If you have a true disability
that's the way God made you. He loves you and we love you too.

May America love God and God Bless you.

BIG BROTHER

He was to me, a perfect big brother: always busy.

He bought a sports car to impress the girls.

One day he said to me, "Do you want to play tennis at the school tennis court?"
I said, "yeh, I guess so." I tried to learn tennis by hitting the
tennis ball against the house. He said, "You can drive."
Then I hopped in his cherry red TR4 that he painted.
When I got in the car he said, "give it what you got". Well it was a
stick shift so I tried not to strip the gears in his cool car.

We played tennis. I always loved playing tennis although I wasn't very good. My brother
aimed his shots right between my eyes. He had his methods. I was just glad to hit the
ball over the net. I made him run! I loved getting outside. He played center for our High
School football team and our team was champion of all the schools in our district. My
brother, to this day is always taking care of things. When Mom was alive and we were
still living at home, he always cheered her up. He tried ham radio and morse code.

I played his cornet. I loved sports and music and I bought a small Honda motor bike. I rode
it to Mrs. Mary's house ten miles to her house to practice *Count Your Many Blessings*.

We won first place.

GOING TO THE HOSPITAL

One day I took my dear husband to the hospital. I drove him to the hospital in our white car. He wore his blue shirt and his black shorts, his leather belt, good shoes. And we waited. We were watching people coming to work. It was about 6:30 A.M. Every time anybody came through the double doors. The doors sounded "Wow" "Wow".

There were some seats and a piano that played by itself. It was a real nice baby grand piano.

I said I'm going to do whatever I had to do to help my husband. It was hard bringing him to the hospital. He's so good natured. I tried to stay calm. He was in the hospital two days.

He had a heart catheter, and blood tests. He is a very kind man and he tried to be as pleasant as he could be. It is so hot in Florida. I take it very hard in the summer. I sure learned my way to the hospital and back home.

The second day his nurse said he had to stay another day. But the angiogram and his blood tests were satisfactory. The Drs. ordered his pills and said he could go home, Yeh! Larry called me about 4:00. So I drove up to the main entrance. Then parked my car nearby and went inside to wait for him. His nurse wheeled him down. She helped him get in the car with his stuff and I drove him home!

LUCKY AND IFFIN

They were left; dumped at a
convenience store near us.
I probably was buying milk.
Well the manager was in stitches!
He said "I cannot take any more stray
cats in my house. He had enough, eight!"

I had been praying for a kitten to get another cat.
So I scooped up Iffin, the long haired grey cat.
He was so cute, and his brother a short haired grey was
yowling at the top of his voice
Out in the middle of the street at a
very busy intersection near here.
Well I chased him out of the street and picked him up too.
They both got in the back window of my car
And I brought them home.

They had a real treat I had thawed and cooked
bait fish for them to eat about a week.
Chew, chew, slurp slurp. They loved it.

About a year later our neighbor gave us some
Delicious canned cat food. And some healthy dry cat food.
And water for them. They didn't want milk. But they needed water
In the summer.

Our daughter brushed the cats, They would protest.
But they loved it.
"Iffin was named because Ifffin he wanted to sit down
anywhere he would and he left cat hair anywhere.
"Lucky" because I saved his life from the middle
Of the street.

So one hot summer day. Sherri our daughter trimmed
Iffin's long fur with a brush and hair clippers.
When she was done we had a "Poodle cut Cat"
Even with his meows and protests. But he felt so much cooler.

Our kittens are gone now but good memories remain.

DOLLY

My name is Dolly and
I'm a spoiled little cat
I'm the pick of the litter but
You can't blame me for that.

My Daddy's a Pershian
Mom's from Siam
When it comes to mealtime.
They're spoiled as I am.

I know what I want
And I know what I like
"Whisker Lickens" in the morning
And the same at night

These moist tender bites
Are the best of the pickins
Mouth watering delight with the "perfect"
Flavor of Whisker Lickins.

Meow

by Jean Spurlock.

Printed in the United States
By Bookmasters